Dear Parent:

Buckle up! You are about to join your child on a very exciting journey. The destination? Independent reading!

Road to Reading will help you and your child get there. The program offers books at five levels, or Miles, that accompany children from their first attempts at reading to successfully reading on their own. Each Mile is paved with engaging stories and delightful artwork.

Getting Started
For children who know the alphabet and are eager to begin reading
• easy words • fun rhythms • big type • picture clues

Reading With Help
For children who recognize some words and sound out others with help
• short sentences • pattern stories • simple plotlines

Reading On Your Own
For children who are ready to read easy stories by themselves
• longer sentences • more complex plotlines • easy dialogue

First Chapter Books
For children who want to take the plunge into chapter books
• bite-size chapters • short paragraphs • full-color art

Chapter Books
For children who are comfortable reading independently
• longer chapters • occasional black-and-white illustrations

There's no need to hurry through the Miles. Road to Reading is designed without age or grade levels. Children can progress at their own speed, developing confidence and pride in their reading ability no matter what their age or grade.

So sit back and enjoy the ride—every Mile of the way!

For my two beautiful nieces, with thanks for
lending me their names
T.J.

For Sylvia and Maddy
F.R.

Library of Congress Cataloging-in-Publication Data
Jordan, Taylor.
Hiccup / by Taylor Jordan ; illustrated by Frank Remkiewicz.
  p.   cm. — (Road to reading. Mile 1)
Summary: With the help of his sister, Hippo tries all sorts of
silly stunts to try to cure his hiccups.
ISBN 0-307-26103-4 (pbk.)
[1. Hippopotamus—Fiction. 2. Hiccups—Fiction. 3. Brothers and
sisters—Fiction.] I. Remkiewicz, Frank, ill. II. Title.
III. Series.
PZ7.J76855 Hi 1998
[E]—dc21
                                              98-12020
                                              CIP
                                              AC

A GOLDEN BOOK • New York
Golden Books Publishing Company, Inc. New York, New York 10106

ISBN: 0-307-26103-4

A MCMXCVIII

HICCUP

by Taylor Jordan
illustrated by Frank Remkiewicz

Hiccup.

Hiccup. Hiccup.

One. Two. Three.

Four. Five. Six.

Seven. Eight. Nine—

Ten!

Hiccup.

Hiccup. Hiccup.

BOO!

Hiccup.

Hiccup.

Hiccup.

Hiccup.

Hiccup?

Cluck, cluck, cluck.

Hooray!

Hiccup.